ALISON HOLST'S
COOKING FOR
CHRISTMAS

CHRISTMAS BAKING & EDIBLE GIFTS

Cooking for Christmas

First published 1995 by Hyndman
Publishing PO Box 5017, Dunedin.
© Text: Alison Holst
Designers: Rob Di Leva
Production: Di Leva Design
Illustrator: Clare Ferguson
Photography: Sal Criscillo
Home Economists: Alison Holst, Jane
Ritchie, Dee Harris
Printing: Tablet Colour Print

COVER PHOTOGRAPH:
Pineapple Christmas Cake
Left to right, Lebkuchen, Herbed Vinegars, Sherried Fruit
Medley, Nuts to Nibble, Christmas Pickle, Apricot Balls,
Traditional Mince Pies.

To me, Christmas means a happy family gathering with excited children, the exchange of pretty gift-wrapped packages beside a decorated tree, and seasonal food to be enjoyed with friends and family.

Although Christmas is a very busy time of year, especially for those organising families and their food, most of us remember fondly the traditional foods which our mothers, aunts and grandmothers produced each year. If you think that these may be outdated, look at the wide range of traditional Christmas foods on sale in good food and gift stores, and you will realise that this is certainly not the case.

After you have admired the store foods in their attractive packaging, take a look at the price tags attached! These will probably make you realise that, by making Christmas treats as gifts for your extended family and friends, you will be giving personalised and practical gifts of considerable worth, which display your skills, and are sure to be used and appreciated.

I hope that the recipes in this book will whet your appetite and inspire you! Many of the foods may be made some time before Christmas, before the inevitable last minute rush. A few recipes require special skills, but many are suitable for children to make by themselves, or with a little help from you. I hope that you will encourage this participation, so that even young children realise that Christmas is a time for shared family activity and hand-made gifts; for giving, as well as receiving!

For maximum impact, present your gifts attractively. Consider reusable containers, such as glasses, decorative jars, baskets and boxes, muffin or cake pans, and even teatowels. Make good use of ribbons and wraps, and don't forget to add creative, informative and fun labels!

I hope that the foods from this book which you cook, enjoy yourself, and give to others, will make Christmas an even happier time for you and your families!

Contents

Before you make…

There's more to a successful Christmas cake than just a recipe! A perfectly reliable recipe can fail if you misinterpret or modify the instructions.

Washing Fruit

It is important that dried fruit is plump, moist and never gritty. I now wash and "plump up" premixed fruit as well as currants, raisins, sultanas, etc. Put the measured fruit into a colander or large sieve, pour boiling water over it, drain well, then dry it in the sun on a teatowel, in a low oven in a roasting pan, or in a microwave oven on paper towels. Unless especially soaked ahead according to your recipe, fruit should be dry, cooled and "plumped" before it is added to the other ingredients. Wash it the day before you plan to make your cake.

Baking Powder

Baking powder and baking soda are not essential in a rich fruit cake. Both make the cake rise slightly. Baking soda tends to make a darker cake.

Curdling

Curdled cake mixtures are said not to have as good a texture as uncurdled mixtures, so avoid curdling if you can. Mixtures often curdle as the eggs are added. You can prevent this by adding 1 - 2 tablespoons of the measured flour between egg additions. Flavourings are often added to the creamed butter and sugar because they blend well when mixed with fat, but these flavoured mixtures tend to curdle more readily than unflavoured ones, so you may choose to add spices with the flour. Do not worry too much about curdling however. I doubt whether most people could tell the difference!

Tin Sizes

In my recipes, the size of tin has been specified. If you use a different tin you may need to alter the cooking time or temperature slightly. If the recipe calls for a 23cm square tin, the same mixture put into a 23cm round tin will make a deeper cake which will take a little longer to cook, and which might cook more evenly at a slightly lower temperature. The same mixture in a 20cm square tin will be the same depth as the 23cm round cake. In a 20cm round tin the cake would be even deeper and need longer cooking.

Papering Tins

If you use a recipe that has been used by your great-grandmother, remember that your stove differs from hers! In our well-regulated ovens you can make an excellent cake in a tin lined with a Teflon liner or *one* layer of greaseproof paper.

...your Christmas Cake

Where and how you store your cake is important. Get it right! Incorrect storage can spoil your cake.
The following guidelines apply to all rich cakes.

Cooking Times

The cooking time given in a recipe can never be exact because different ovens have different characteristics. Use the given time as a guide only - look at, and test your cake during the last hour of cooking. When ready, the cake will have shrunk slightly from the edge of the tin and be firm in the middle. A skewer pushed into the middle should come out clean with no uncooked mixture on it. Never leave a rich cake to turn itself off in an automatic oven. A cake which sinks in the middle on cooling is probably not cooked right through.

Splits and Peaks

If you have baked your cake previously and found that it splits and peaks during baking, use ¼–½ cup less flour, or a larger tin, or a lower oven temperature. I do not like to advise major alterations in rich cake recipe proportions but think you are better to try another recipe.

Maturing and Storage

Make your cake several weeks before you need it so it has time to mature and store it properly.

Cakes should not be stored in completely airtight containers unless they are to be refrigerated or frozen. (Rich cakes freeze well up to 6 months.)

Cakes stored at room temperature may go mouldy when stored in airtight plastic bags, aluminium foil, or airtight plastic boxes.

Use greaseproof paper, clean tea towels and non-airtight metal cake tins which allow some air circulation. In these, a rich cake should not go mouldy as it can in an airtight container.

Alcohol

Some cake recipes call for sherry or other spirits added to the raw mixture. Other recipes call for spirits to be poured or sprinkled over the cake when it is taken from the oven. This won't hurt the cake as long as it is cooked! Put more round the edges than you put in the middle.

First Aid for Dry Cakes

Brush all cake surfaces liberally with sherry brandy/or spirits. Place cake in a plastic bag and refrigerate for at least a day. Repeat applications until the cake is as moist as you like it!

To Decorate...

You want to make your Christmas cake look as attractive as possible. Decide how you want to decorate it before you put it in the oven. You have several options:

• Place nuts and/or crystallised cherries on the surface of the cake before you bake it. Place them at random, or arrange in a pattern. Use plump and perfect nuts. Brush with lightly beaten egg 15 minutes before baking for a glossy finish.

• You can stick halved or sliced nuts and pieces of crystallised fruit on the surface of an undecorated, nearly cooked cake, if you brush its surface with golden syrup, or a thick sugar syrup half an hour before the cake is cooked. Quickly place the fruit and nuts in place, then brush the whole surface with thinned syrup two or three times during the next half hour.

• Cakes decorated like this should have an attractive shiny surface, which will look good with a paper frill or a wide ribbon around the cake. Place a sprig of holly, or a Christmas ornament in the centre. Marzipan fruit piled on top also looks pretty (see page 46).

• Cakes which are to be iced should be brought to room temperature first. The first coating is usually a layer of almond icing, which is rolled out then laid on the cake which has been brushed with jam, so the icing sticks to it. This coat ensures that the top layer of icing is not discoloured by the cake and makes the top layer more smooth.

• The top coat may be made of bought or homemade "plastic" icing. This is rolled out and placed on top of the almond icing, which should be moistened with a little water or sugar syrup. The idea is to finish up with a smooth surface, so cut off overhanging pieces, rather than folding them over.

Royal icing may be used as a top coat instead of plastic icing. Decorations are usually made of almond icing or royal icing.

Home made Almond Icing

Almond icing is easy to make. This is enough for a medium sized cake. Double the quantity if you want enough for a very thick layer, for icing down the sides, or for marzipan fruit.

100g ground almonds
1 cup icing sugar
$\frac{1}{2}$ cup caster sugar
1 egg yolk
2 Tbsp lemon juice, strained
$\frac{1}{4}$ tsp almond essence (optional)

Combine the ground almonds and sugars in a food processor or mixing bowl. Mix the egg yolk with half of the lemon juice and add to the almond mixture with a little almond essence if desired.

Add remaining lemon juice, a little at a time, until you make a paste that is easy to roll out.

...your Christmas Cake

Home-made Almond Icing may be used in two places on a cake. Use it for a layer under the top coat of icing, and make decorations with it too.

Warm a little apricot jam, sieve, and brush over the cake, then roll out the almond paste on a dry board sprinkled with icing sugar. Place over the cake smoothly, using a rolling pin.

Plastic Icing

Plastic icing is not really difficult to make yourself, but is best not attempted by an inexperienced cook.

1 Tbsp gelatine
3 Tbsp cold water
3 Tbsp liquid glucose
2 tsp glycerine
1 kg icing sugar

Mix the gelatine and cold water, stand for 3–4 minutes, then warm in a microwave or over low heat, only until the gelatine has dissolved.

Sift the icing sugar into a large bowl, pour the lukewarm gelatine mixture into the centre of it, then mix it with a dough hook or a wooden spoon. As soon as reasonably firm, mix with your hands until you have a smooth, workable, dough (you may need to add a little hot water). Roll out on a board dusted with icing sugar, and place over moistened almond icing. Prick any air bubbles with a needle, and put a smooth surface on the icing by polishing it with a square of smooth, shiny card. As you rub the card around and around, you will find that a lovely, smooth, shiny surface forms.

Royal Icing

The top coat of icing on a fruit cake is sometimes made of Royal icing, rather than plastic icing. Royal icing is very white, sets hard and is easy to pipe into rosettes, lines, dots, etc. for decorations, too.

1 egg white
1 tsp lemon juice, strained
½ tsp glycerine (optional)
2 cups sifted icing sugar

In a food processor or bowl, mix the egg white and lemon juice only until frothy. Add the icing sugar a few tablespoons at a time, mixing well between additions. Stop when the icing is the consistency you want. Mix in glycerine.

Use the icing immediately, or store it in an airtight bag for up to two or three days. For piping, thin down with a little water if necessary.

Notes: If you want to pipe royal icing into elaborate shapes such as leaves and roses, buy icing sugar which does not contain cornflour. Glycerine is supposed to keep royal icing softer than it would be otherwise, but it is not essential.

Pineapple Christmas Cake

For many years my rich pineapple cake has been made to celebrate Christmas, by families all around the country. It is the most used of all my rich cake recipes.

For 1 23cm cake, 2 18cm cakes or 12 (mini) 10cm cakes:

*1.5kg mixed fruit ***
450g can crushed pineapple
3 cups flour
1 tsp each cinnamon and mixed spice
1/2 tsp ground cloves
225g butter
1 cup sugar
1/2 tsp each vanilla, almond and lemon essences
6 large eggs
up to 1 extra cup of flour
about 50g glace cherries and 50g blanched almonds for decoration

* *Choose only very good quality mixed fruit. If this is not available replace with 700g sultanas, 500g raisins, 250g currants and 50g mixed peel.*

Two or three days before mixing the cake, put the mixed fruit in a large (unperforated) oven bag or plastic bag with the undrained pineapple. Leave in a warm place, turning bag occasionally, until all the juice is absorbed.

Note: To make cake immediately, discard liquid from pineapple. Wash, then dry fruit the same day that you mix the cake. You are unlikely to need the extra flour.

To make the cake:

Mix the spices with 3 cups of flour and put aside. Cream the butter, sugar and essences until light and smooth. Beat in eggs, one at a time, adding about 2 tablespoons of the spiced flour with each egg. Toss together the prepared fruit and the remaining spiced flour in a large bowl or a roasting pan. Stir in the creamed mixture using a wooden spoon or your hand.

Mixture should be just soft enough to drop from your hand. If it seems too soft, add more flour. Press mixture into paper-lined tin(s), levelling the top(s).

Decorate with blanched almonds and cherries if you do not plan to ice the cake.

• Bake 23cm cake at 150°C for 1½ hours, then at 130°C for about 2 hours longer.

• Bake 18cm cakes at 140°C for 1 hour, then at 130°C for about an hour longer.

• Bake mini cakes (225–250g each) at 130°C for about 1½ hours. (Use paper-lined, well cleaned fish cans.)

Cakes are cooked when a skewer pushed to base of middle of the cake comes out clean (see page 4). Sprinkle hot cake(s) with about ¼ cup brandy or sherry, if you like. Remove cake(s) from tin(s) when cold.

Peter's Special Cake

This is a lovely, dark, moist, fruity cake. It contains no essences. I like to add a mixture of spices, but I don't use very much of any one of these. You can leave out those you do not have.

For 1 23cm square or round cake:

500g sultanas
500g raisins
500g currants
½ cup sherry
rind of 1 lemon
rind of 1 orange
1½ cups brown sugar
250g butter, softened
1 Tbsp treacle
5 eggs
2 cups flour
*½ tsp each ground allspice, cardamom,
     cinnamon, cloves, coriander and
     nutmeg*

One to two days before cake is made, put the dried fruits into a plastic bag with the sherry. Turn the bag every now and then. Leave the bag in a warm place, until all the sherry has been absorbed by the fruit.

Remove coloured rind of lemon and orange with a potato peeler. Process with the sugar until very finely chopped. Add butter, process until soft and fluffy then add the treacle and mix again. Add eggs, one at a time, with a tablespoon of the measured flour between each. Mix the rest of the flour and the spices with the fruit, in a very large bowl.

Tip the creamed mixture into the floured fruit, and mix until soft enough to drop from your hand. If the mixture is too dry, add up to ¼ cup of extra sherry or spirits.

Put the mixture into a 23cm round or square tin (see page 4) lined with greaseproof paper. Decorate top with almonds or cherries if you like.

Bake at 150°C for 1 hour, then at 140°C for about 3 hours, until a skewer in the centre comes out clean.

Dribble ¼ cup of rum or brandy over it while it is very hot, if you like.

Leave an hour before removing from the tin.

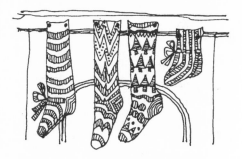

Love Cake

This is an unusual moist, rich cake, quite light in colour. It takes some time and care to assemble all the ingredients. I make it with love for the people I care about and have named it accordingly.

For 1 23cm square cake:

1kg sultanas
150g mixed peel
150g cherries
½ cup rum, brandy or whisky
1–2 tsp vanilla essence
1–2 tsp almond essence
1 tsp lemon essence
1 tsp ground cardamom
1 tsp cinnamon
1 tsp grated nutmeg
½ tsp ground cloves
¼ cup strawberry jam
¼ cup apricot jam
125g butter
1 cup sugar
5 eggs
½ cup semolina
2 cups ground almonds
1¼ cups self-raising flour

Put the sultanas, mixed peel and cherries in a large mixing bowl. Add the spirits of your choice and mix thoroughly with the fruit, breaking up any lumps. Add the essences, using the larger quantities for more pronounced flavour, then add the spices. Measure the jams, using no more than half a cup in total. Warm together until they are quite runny, but do not boil. Add to the fruit, then mix everything together well using your hands.

Cover the bowl tightly with plastic film, and leave it to stand in a warm room for 36 hours. Stir the mixture several times during this period.

Cream the softened but not melted butter with the sugar. Add the eggs one at a time, alternately with tablespoons of the measured semolina. Next beat in the ground almonds, then the flour. Mix thoroughly but do not over mix. Tip this mixture into the bowl of marinated fruit and mix well with your hands.

Preheat the oven to 160°C. Spread mixture into a prepared 23cm square cake tin, pushing it into the corners and levelling the top. Decorate with blanched almonds and cherries if you do not intend to ice the cake.

Turn oven down to 150°C when you put the cake into it. Bake at 150°C for 1 hour then at 140°C for 1–2 hours or until the centre feels firm and a skewer comes out clean.

Cathedral Cake

This spectacular and decorative cake is made mainly of nuts and glace fruit! It requires no icing or other decoration. When sliced thinly and held up to the light, it resembles a stained glass window.

For 1 20cm ring cake or 2 small loaves:

1 cup brazil nuts
½ cup blanched almonds
½ cup cashew nuts
1 cup red cherries
½ cup mixed cherries
1 cup glace fruit, eg pineapple, mangoes, peaches, apricots
1 cup dried fruit
¾ cup flour
½ cup brown sugar
¼ tsp cinnamon
½ tsp baking powder
½ tsp salt
2 eggs
½ tsp vanilla essence

Measure the nuts, fruit and dry ingredients into a large bowl, reserving some for decoration. Cut up large pieces of fruit, but leave some long thin pieces if desired, especially if using mango.

Mix eggs and vanilla until thoroughly combined and add to the other ingredients. Mix thoroughly by hand.

Press evenly into a 20cm ring tin, or two small loaf tins, each lined with a teflon liner or sprayed baking paper to prevent sticking. Press reserved cherries and nuts into the top for decoration.

Bake at 130°C for 2 hours or until firm in centre. Cool, remove from tin and peel away liner(s). Brush all over with rum, brandy, or whisky. Store at room temperature in greaseproof paper or refrigerate in plastic wrap. This cake keeps well for several months. Cut into thin slices with a serrated knife.

Easy-mix Fruit and Rum Cake

Here is a cake of modest size, which is very little trouble to put together. Its wonderful flavour comes from the dark raisins and the rum used in it - it contains no essences or spices at all.

For 1 20cm square or round cake:

1 kg small dark (Californian) raisins
½ cup liquid (see below)
200g butter
2 cups flour
1 cup sugar
1 tsp baking soda
½ tsp salt
¼ cup golden syrup
½ cup milk
2 large eggs

Put the raisins in an unpunctured plastic bag with ½ cup of rum or a mixture of sherry and rum and leave the fruit to stand in it for 24–48 hours, until the fruit has soaked up all the liquid.

Cut or rub the cold butter into the flour, sugar, baking soda and salt, using a food processor, a pastry blender, or your fingers.

Measure the syrup in a measure preheated with very hot water, warm the syrup and milk just enough to combine them, beat in the eggs, then mix this liquid, the prepared fruit and the dry mixture together.

If you do not intend to ice your cake, decorate the top with a pattern of blanched almonds, cherries, etc.

Bake in a lined 20cm square tin at 150°C

for 2¼–2 ½ hours, until a skewer inserted in the centre, pushed down to the bottom, comes out clean.

If you have decorated the top of the cake with nuts, "polish" them by rubbing a little oil on the palm of your hand, and rubbing your hand over the surface of the cake until the nuts shine.

Easy-Mix Christmas Cake

Kirsten's Christmas Loaf

Kirsten's Christmas Loaf

This loaf looks festive, is relatively quick to make and the recipe produces a large number of pieces.
A few slices in a small cellophane bag, tied with pretty curling ribbon, make a good small gift.

Makes a loaf 9 x 23cm:

3 eggs
½ tsp salt
½ cup sugar
¼ tsp almond essence
½ tsp vanilla essence
finely grated rind of 1 orange
1 cup flour
1½ cups raw almonds
1½ cups red glace cherries

Beat eggs, salt, sugar and essences until light and fluffy, then add the finely grated orange rind.

Mix the flour, almonds and cherries together, then fold them into the egg mixture.

Turn mixture into a loaf tin about 9x23x8 cm, lined with a Teflon liner or buttered baking paper, making sure that the top is evenly flattened. Bake at 180°C for 45–50 minutes, or until loaf is lightly browned and the centre springs back when pressed.

When cool remove from tin, wrap and refrigerate for at least 24 hours, then cut into about 40 thin slices with a sharp, serrated knife.

Bake slices on a lined oven tray at 125°–150°C for about 30 minutes, until the slices colour slightly. Cool on racks then store in airtight containers until required.

Note: If you want a multi-coloured loaf, use cherries of mixed colours, some red and some green.

If you use unblanched almonds, they will be more noticeable in the loaf.

Italian Festive Cake

This is an unusual, flat, dark, dense, chocolately cake which needs to be cut in small slivers with a very sharp knife. Although my version is chewier than the original it is absolutely delicious and worth making.

For a 20cm cake:

¾ cup whole, blanched almonds

¾ cup hazelnuts

¾ cup roasted cashew or pistachio nuts

½ cup prunes

½ cup apricots

½ cup glace pineapple

½ cup mixed peel

½ cup flour

2 Tbsp cocoa

1 tsp cinnamon

1 tsp mixed spice

½ cup sugar

½ cup honey

½ cup chocolate chips

2 Tbsp icing sugar

Spread the almonds and hazelnuts in a single layer on an oven tray and cook at 180°C for about 10 minutes or until lightly browned. Remove from the oven, cool, chop roughly with the other nuts in a food processor, then put into a large mixing bowl.

Without washing the food processor bowl, add the dried fruit and chop briefly. Add to the chopped nuts in the bowl.

Sift over the fruit and nuts the flour, cocoa and spices and mix to coat.

Measure into a small pot the sugar and honey and over low heat stir until well mixed then leave to simmer for about 5 minutes or until a little of the syrup forms a "soft ball" when dropped into cold water. Remove immediately from the heat and stir in the chocolate chips. Stir to combine then pour onto the fruit and nut mixture and mix well.

Line a 20cm cake tin with a Teflon liner or sprayed baking paper to cover the bottom of the tin and to come 3cm up the sides of the tin. Working quickly tip the mixture into the prepared tin pressing it down well. Cook for about 35 minutes at 150°C or until the centre feels as firm as the edges.

Remove from the tin when cold, wrap in foil and leave for at least 24 hours before cutting the cake in half, then quarters. Cut each quarter in long, thin, parallel strips.

To serve sprinkle lightly with icing sugar.

Almond Ring

*Here is something festive to serve with coffee after dinner, or with drinks. It looks pretty, and makes
an attractive gift, especially if you stand it on a round board or plate and wrap it in clear film.*

200g flaky or puff pastry
1½ cups ground almonds
¾ cup sugar
½ tsp grated lemon rind
½ tsp almond essence
1 large egg
12 red crystallised cherries
1 cup apricot jam
angelica or green cherries

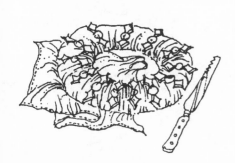

Roll the pastry out thinly to a long thin rectangle 60cm and 12cm wide.

Measure the next four ingredients into a bowl. Beat the egg to combine the white and yolk, then add half of it to the almond mixture. Mix well. Add more egg until the almond mixture is moist enough to roll. Reserve about a teaspoonful of egg to glaze the pastry. If the mixture still looks dry, beat a second egg, and add a little of this.

Either roll the almond mixture into a long thin roll (the length of the pastry) or put it on the pastry in small blobs, and shape it into a roll with damp hands. Halve all the cherries. Press sixteen of the halves into the almond mixture, and pinch the almond mixture over them. Moisten the far side of the pastry with water.

Fold the undampened side of pastry over the almond mixture. Fold the pastry-coated almond mixture over the dampened pastry, then bring the ends round in a circle, so the visible long join of the pastry is on the inside, not the outside of the circle. Pinch the joined edges together firmly.

Transfer onto a lightly buttered (or sprayed) oven slide. Brush with lightly beaten egg. Do not prick the pastry.

Bake at 220°C for 10–15 minutes, or until pastry is evenly golden brown.

Remove from oven and brush immediately with apricot jam. Decorate top with remaining cherry halves and angelica, and replace in the oven for about 2 minutes.

Note: If you do not like traditional Christmas cake, consider making almond rings instead, freezing them until close to the time you want them.

Holiday Surprise Cake

Although I am especially partial to the almond and apricot filling given here, I make this cake over the Christmas period with spoonfuls of Christmas mincemeat dropped into it, and find that this variation is very popular, too.

Filling:

about 6 dried apricots

about 10 almonds

1/4 cup coconut

3 Tbsp sugar

1/4 cup sherry or orange juice

few drops almond essence (optional)

Cake:

1/2 cup sour cream

1 egg

1/2 cup sugar

few drops each of vanilla and almond
    essence

1 cup self-raising flour

1/8 tsp baking soda

1/4 tsp salt

1 Tbsp orange juice or milk

First make the filling by putting the dried apricots, almonds, coconut and sugar in a food processor and chopping finely. Add the sherry and essence, process again, briefly, then remove the mixture, which now sticks together, from the food processor, using a rubber scraper. The machine should be almost clean.

To make the cake: Measure into the unwashed processor the sour cream, egg, sugar and essences. Process briefly to mix, then add the remaining ingredients, unsifted, and process briefly again, just enough to mix in the flour. The mixture should be runnier than a normal cake mixture. Pour it into a well buttered or sprayed 20cm ring tin 35mm high, with a paper-lined bottom. Drop teaspoonfuls of the filling evenly over the batter, without letting it touch the sides.

Bake at 190°C for about 25 minutes, or until top is golden brown, and centre feels firm when pressed. As the cake bakes the filling sinks, and should be completely, or nearly all covered by the batter. Leave to stand on a rack for about 5 minutes, then run a knife around the tin, and turn out carefully.

Serve warm or cold, preferably soon after baking, dusted with icing sugar.

Yeasty Wreath

Although few of us make bread regularly, many of us like to make something yeasty for special
occasions. Here is a loaf which you may like to make and bake, one day during the Christmas break.

2 tsp dried yeast
1 Tbsp sugar
50g butter
1 cup milk
1–1½ tsp salt
3 cups flour

Filling :

50g butter
¼ cup flour
2 Tbsp sugar
½ cup blanched roasted almonds
¼ cup red glace cherries, chopped
¼ cup green glace cherries, chopped
½ cup dried apricots, chopped
¾ tsp almond essence

Icing:

1 cup icing sugar
2 Tbsp lemon juice

Mix the dry yeast granules, sugar and ½ cup of warm water in a large mixing bowl. Leave to stand in a warm place for a few minutes until it is frothy.

Melt the butter, add the milk and salt and warm to blood heat, then tip this into the bubbly yeast mixture. Stir in 2½ cups of the flour. Beat vigorously for at least 10 seconds, cover the bowl with plastic film and leave to rise in a warm place until twice original volume.

Beat in the remaining flour, adding a little more if necessary, to make a dough just firm enough to knead. Keep the board and your hands floured enough to stop the dough sticking. Knead until smooth and satiny, add flour only if dough sticks.

Roll out into a rectangle 25 x 25 cm on a well floured surface.

To make the filling: Soften the butter. Beat in the flour and sugar, then add the chopped almonds, cherries, apricots and almond essence.

Dot the filling evenly over the dough surface, then roll dough tightly, starting from a long edge.

Cut the roll in half lengthwise using a sharp knife, then twist the two strands loosely together, keeping cut side out. Form into a ring, pinching ends together, on a floured baking tray. Leave to rise in a warm place. Brush lightly with egg wash (1 egg beaten with 1 Tbsp water) for a glazed surface if desired. Bake at 200° C for 20 minutes or until lightly browned.

While warm drizzle with icing made by combining icing sugar and lemon juice.

Elaine's Christmas Pudding

These puddings are traditionally wrapped in calico, tightly tied and slowly boiled in a pot of water, but you may cook them in covered pudding bowls (for 3 hours) if preferred.

For 8 –10 servings:

2 cups flour
1 cup brown sugar
2 tsp baking soda
2 tsp mixed spice
2 tsp cinnamon
½ tsp ground cloves
6 cups (about 950g) mixed fruit
2 cups Californian dark raisins
grated rind of 1 orange
2 eggs
125g butter, melted
½ cup liquid*

* *We used Emerson's London Porter from the Dunedin Boutique Brewery. Other suggestions are: stout, sherry, gingerale, or orange juice.*

Measure the dry ingredients and spices into a large bowl, toss together to mix. Add the fruit and mix with your hands, ensuring that the fruit is well coated with the flour. Add the rind, lightly beaten eggs, melted butter and the liquid of your choice, mix well.

Cut closely woven (unbleached) calico into squares about 60cm square for 2 large puddings, or into 45cm squares for 6 smaller puddings (which make lovely gifts) and rinse thoroughly in hot water. Squeeze dry, then flatten out on the bench. (It is not necessary to flour the surface of the cloth.) Put pudding mixture into the centre of a cloth and mould into a round shape. Gather the calico evenly around the pudding and tie tightly with string leaving a gap of about 3 cm to allow room for the pudding to expand as it cooks. Tie the ends of the string to form a loop so you can hang up the pudding to dry after cooking.

Put one or more puddings in a big pot large enough to allow the puddings to "float" and move freely. The pot should be about three quarters full of rapidly boiling water to seal the outside of the pudding as soon as possible. Turn the heat down to simmer, cover and leave to boil for 3–4 hours depending on size. During this time check frequently to see that there is sufficient water in the pot. Remove the puddings from the pot at the end of the cooking time and hang from hooks or a broom handle in a cool place to dry.

To store: Refrigerate or hang in a cool dry place for up to 3 months.

To reheat: Simmer pudding in bag for 2–3 hours. Unwrap and leave to stand for 15–30 minutes before serving.

Marion's Oaty Pudding

This rich steamed pudding is an interesting one because it contains no flour, and no butter or oil. It has a lovely flavour, a really good, dark colour, and a wonderful aroma.

For 4–6 servings:

1 cup (fine) rolled oats
1 cup milk
400–425g mixed fruit
1 egg
2 household dessertspoons golden syrup
1 tsp baking soda
1 tsp cinnamon
1 tsp mixed spice
½ tsp ground cloves
½ tsp lemon essence

Measure the rolled oats into a mixing bowl, and pour the milk over. Leave to stand for 5 minutes.

Put the dried fruit into a sieve and run hot water over it, then leave it to drain.

Add the egg and golden syrup to the rolled oats mixture. Beat with a fork to mix well. Stir the cleaned, drained fruit into the oat mixture with the fork, then sprinkle the soda and spices over all this. Add the lemon essence, and stir just enough to mix everything. If the mixture is so wet that some thin liquid separates from the main mixture, add another 2 tablespoons of rolled oats, and leave it to stand a few minutes longer.

To cook conventionally: Pour the mixture into a 4 cup bowl that has been well buttered or sprayed, and which has had its bottom lined with a circle of baking paper. Stand the uncovered bowl on a saucer or small rack in a saucepan half full of boiling water. Cover tightly, and simmer for 2½–3 hours, adding more boiling water if necessary.

Leave to stand for 5 minutes, run a knife around the bowl, and turn out the pudding.

To microwave: Line the bottom of a small microwave ring pan with a Teflon ring pan liner, or a circle of baking paper. Pour the pudding mixture into this, and cover with cling wrap. Pierce a few holes in this, and cook on Medium for 12–15 minutes, until the mixture close to the central ring springs back when pressed. Leave to stand for 5 minutes, before turning out onto a plate.

Serve with Sauce (see page 25).

Traditional Christmas Pudding

This recipe is similar to one made by my mother and my aunts. Make it well in advance (freezing it if you like) and have it ready to boil up again on Christmas Day.

For 8 - 12 servings:

2 cups flour
¾ cup suet OR 75g butter
½ cup brown sugar
1 cup raisins
1 cup currants
1 cup sultanas
¼ cup mixed peel
¼ cup cherries
1 tsp cinnamon
1 tsp mixed spice
½ cup golden syrup
½ cup milk
1 tsp baking soda
2 eggs
grated rind of 1 orange
grated rind of 1 lemon

Mix together in a large basin the flour, suet and brown sugar. If using butter rub it into the flour. Add this to the fruit which has been washed, then dried in the oven or another warm place. Stir in the spices.

Warm the golden syrup, and add it to the milk with the baking soda dissolved in it, the eggs and the finely grated citrus rind. Beat with a fork until well mixed. Pour the egg mixture into the dry ingredients and fruit. Mix well.

Butter or spray a large basin and pour the mixture into it, leaving enough space for the pudding to rise as it cooks. Cover the basin with its lid or several layers of greaseproof paper tied firmly in place with string, or with foil. Place on a rack or a saucer in a large saucepan, half filled with boiling water. Put a lid on the saucepan and boil gently for 3–4 hours.

Check frequently to see that the pudding has not boiled dry. When necessary, add more boiling water.

After the pudding has boiled, remove it from its basin and leave to cool on a wire rack. When cold wrap in aluminium foil or a plastic bag and keep it in a cool dry place until it is needed. (I store my pudding in the bottom of the refrigerator).

When the pudding is to be used, unwrap it, sprinkle it with sherry, whisky or brandy, replace it in the basin with a tight covering and steam it again for 1–3 hours (the longer the better).

Serve hot with the sauce of your choice (see page 25).

Traditional Christmas Pudding

Festive Wreath

To serve your Christmas Pudding

To "flame" a Christmas Pudding, heat 1-2 tablespoons of brandy, whisky or rum to bath temperature. Pour it over the hot pudding and set alight. The brandy will not burn unless it is heated first. (The flame may not be visible unless the room is in darkness).

Mary Alice's Rum Butter

This delicious "sauce" makes any steamed pudding very special! Try it as a topping for mincemeat pies or muffins too. Make extra, for gifts for good friends!

100g softened butter
1 cup brown sugar
1 tsp freshly grated nutmeg
2 Tbsp rum

Beat or process all the ingredients until light and creamy. Cover and refrigerate to store for up to a month.

Serve at room temperature.

Brandy Butter (Hard Sauce)

This very rich sauce should be eaten in small amounts!

125g softened butter
2 cups icing sugar
1 Tbsp brandy

Beat or process all ingredients until light and creamy. Refrigerate, until the butter hardens. Pile into a serving dish and serve at room temperature. For individual servings, chill the mixture until easy to handle, roll into walnut-sized balls, then refrigerate until required.

Variation: For hard sauce with a slightly grainy texture, replace the icing sugar with 1 cup of caster sugar.

Creamy Custard Sauce

A less rich alternative!

¼ cup custard powder
¼ cup brown sugar
1 egg
3 cups milk
1 tsp vanilla
2 Tbsp butter
1 Tbsp brandy or 2 Tbsp rum (optional)

Stir custard powder and sugar together in a pot. Add the egg and mix again.

Stir in milk and vanilla, cook over a medium heat, stirring constantly. When the milk is hot, add the butter. As soon as the custard thickens and bubbles, remove from the heat and add the brandy. Serve warm.

Christmas Mincemeats

I've never yet seen bought Christmas Mincemeat which could hold a candle to the three mixtures I make myself.

Traditional Mincemeat

I have made this easy recipe ever since I bought my first food processor. It is a modification of my mother's recipe, but contains no suet, so it can be eaten raw as well as cooked.

rind of 1 lemon
rind of 1 orange
1 cup brown sugar
3 small sturmer apples
juice of 1 lemon
2 cups sultanas
2 cups mixed fruit
1 tsp cinnamon
1 tsp mixed spice
1 tsp grated nutmeg
1 tsp salt
½ tsp ground cloves
¼ cup brandy, whisky or rum

Remove all the coloured rind from the lemon and orange with a potato peeler, then chop with the sugar in the food processor until very fine.

Add the chunks of unpeeled apple, lemon juice, half the sultanas and half the mixed fruit. Process until apple is finely chopped.

Add remaining fruit and flavourings, and process again, briefly without mushing.

Spoon into jars which have been boiled for 3–4 minutes, and top with a little more spirits. Top with boiled screw tops, and refrigerate up to a year, adding more spirits if the mixture becomes dry.

Cooked Mincemeat

This mincemeat is a thickened mixture. I like it because it does not soak into the pastry or filo pastry. Pies, tarts, or triangles will remain crisp a lot longer.

75g-100g butter
1 cup brown sugar
1 tsp mixed spice
½ tsp cinnamon
¼ tsp ground cloves
2 eggs, beaten slightly
2 cups currants
¼–½ cup mixed peel
½ orange, rind and juice
2 apples, finely chopped OR 1 cup drained canned apple
2 Tbsp sherry
2–3 Tbsp spirits

Christmas Mincemeats

For a change, try this light coloured, fresh flavoured fruity mixture on ice cream or as a sweet filling in pies and other pastries.

Melt the butter in a microwave dish or in a metal bowl standing over a pot of boiling water. Stir in the next eight ingredients. Chop, coarsely grate or process the unskinned apple. Stir in with the sherry.

Microwave on High for about 8 minutes or simmer over boiling water 20–30 minutes, stirring regularly. The mixture thickens when cooked. Cool, add the brandy, and store in the refrigerator.

Use as a filling or spread.

Sherried Fruit Medley

This delicious mixture is like a lightly thickened Christmas Mincemeat made from apples, pears and apricots. It has a gold colour and a tangy fruit flavour. Small jars of this mixture, attractively packed and labelled, make unusual and welcome gifts.

*1 cup fruit medley ***
1/2 cup banana chips (or extra fruit medley)
about 1/4 cup pine nuts or chopped almonds
1/2 –1 cup orange juice
1/2 –1 cup white table wine
6 cloves OR 1/8 tsp ground cloves
1 cinnamon stick OR 1/2 tsp ground cinnamon
1/4 –1/2 cup sugar
1/4 –1/2 cup sherry (or brandy or rum)

*   You can make your own fruit mixture by tossing together chopped dried apples, dried apricots, and sultanas. I buy a similar mixture called "Fruit Medley", from the whole (or bulk) food section of my supermarket.

Put the fruit medley into a medium-sized pot. Crush banana chips and add them and the nuts to the fruit.

Make up one and a half cups of liquid, using the orange juice and wine in any proportions you like, then add this and the spices to the fruit, bring to the boil and simmer for 5 minutes.

Remove from the heat, stir in the amount of sugar you want, and leave to cool. Add the sherry, the spirits, or a mixture of the two, and spoon the mixture into a jar.

Refrigerate for up to three months, stirring in extra juice, wine, sherry or spirits if the fruit looks too thick, or if the fruit on top looks as if it is drying out. This mixture makes a good ice-cream topping, a delicious filling for rolled or folded crepes, and an interesting filling for sweet filo triangles.

Christmas Mince Pies

If you have time, turn some of your Christmas Mincemeat into Mince Pies before you get too busy with other Festive tasks, and hide them in the freezer. When time is short, make Filo Triangles instead.

Traditional Mince Pies

This mixture is easy to work with, although it takes some time to shape. It makes pies that freeze and reheat well.

Pastry
100 g butter
½ cup sugar
1 egg
1 cup flour
1 cup self-raising flour

Soften but do not melt butter. Beat in sugar and egg until well combined. Stir in unsifted flours and mix well to form a dough. If too dry, add a little milk. If too soft to work with, refrigerate rather than adding more flour.

Lightly flour a board, to prevent sticking and roll out the pastry.

Using a glass, round lid or fluted cutter, cut out the circles for the bottom of the pies (size will depend on the muffin pans in which the pies will be baked). The circles for the tops are cut with a smaller cutter or, if available, small biscuit cutters which form hearts, stars, diamonds etc.

Ease the dough into (medium or mini) muffin pans, then spoon in the mincemeat mixture of your choice (page 26) and top with the smaller shapes or circles of pastry, pressing the edges lightly.

Bake at 170°–180°C for 10–15 minutes, removing from the oven as soon as the edges start to brown. Cool for 2–3 minutes before carefully lifting from the tins onto cooling racks.

Serve warm, dusted with icing sugar.

Filo Mincemeat Triangles

Each Christmas I make one large batch of traditional mince pies, followed by many of these quick triangles. For best results use thickened fillings (pages 26, 27) unless the triangles will be eaten soon after they are cooked.

Lightly brush with melted butter then stack three sheets of fresh filo pastry. Cut crosswise into 3–5 strips. At one end of each strip put a spoonful of Mincemeat. Fold the filo over the filling forming a triangle. Keep folding to form triangular pastries, enclosing filling completely. Brush with more melted butter.

(See folding instructions on next page.)

Bake at 180°C for about 10 minutes or until golden brown. Serve warm rather than hot, dusted with icing sugar.

Christmas Mincemeat Muffins

Although mince pies are nice, making their crust can be time consuming especially when there are other Christmas chores waiting. Why not put spoonfuls of mixture in muffins instead. Serve these warm, and wait for the compliments!

For 12 medium muffins:

1¾ cups self-raising flour
¾ cup caster sugar
½ tsp salt
2 eggs
½ cup sour cream
½ cup milk
½ tsp rum, whisky or brandy essence
½ cup Christmas Mincemeat (page 26)

Measure the first three ingredients into a large bowl.

In another bowl mix together with a whisk, until smooth, the eggs, sour cream, milk and essence of your choice.

Without overmixing add the liquids to the dry ingredients. Coat 12 medium sized muffin pans with non-stick spray and half fill the 12 pans with the mixture. Using a dampened teaspoon, make a small indentation on the top of each, and into it put 1–2 teaspoons of the mincemeat. Cover each with a spoonful of the remaining mixture trying to cover the "enclosed" mincemeat.

Bake at 200°C for about 12–15 minutes or until golden brown. The centres should spring back when pressed.

Serve warm, for Christmas Day breakfast or brunch, or with coffee at any time of the day over the holiday period. Serve hot for dessert between Christmas and New Year with fresh berries and icecream or whipped cream or with Rum or Brandy Butters (see page 25).

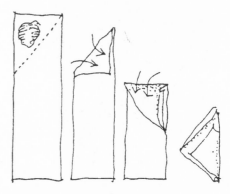

Shaping filo mincemeat triangles

Shortbread Shapes

Shortbread, with its distinctive texture and buttery flavour, is a traditional Christmas treat. When you use decorative cutters instead of making squares or rectangles, your shortbread will be extra special!

220g butter
¹/₂ cup caster sugar
2 cups sifted flour
1 cup cornflour, stirred

Cream the butter, then add the caster sugar and beat until light and fluffy. Sift the flour before measuring it, then spoon it lightly into the cup measure, without packing it down. Add with the cornflour to the creamed mixture, mix thoroughly then chill the dough if it is too soft to roll.

Roll out on a floured board, 7.5mm–1cm thick.

Cut into shapes with cutters, or into rectangles, rounds (with the top of a glass) and squares, and bake on baking paper or a Teflon liner, at 150°C for 15–20 minutes. Watch carefully towards the end of the cooking time and take shortbread from the oven as soon as the edges change colour slightly.

Cool on a rack. Store in airtight containers when cold. Freeze if keeping for more than two weeks before giving away as a gift.

For a relatively inexpensive and attractive presentation, arrange shortbread on a Christmassy paper plate (with or without a doily) then slip the plate into a cellophane "envelope" which you can seal completely with transparent tape.

Lucy's Florentines

There is something wickedly sinful about these rich biscuits. Set in a thin, brandy-snap biscuit are slivered almonds, sliced cherries, and peel. When the biscuits are turned over, you find that their bottoms are spread with melted dark chocolate! Wonderful!

For 16 biscuits:

50g butter, softened
¼ cup brown sugar
3 Tbsp flour
¼ cup flaked almonds
2 Tbsp red glace cherries, chopped
2 Tbsp green glace cherries, chopped
2 Tbsp chopped peel
about 100g dark chocolate

Soften, but do not melt the butter in a small mixing bowl. Add the brown sugar and flour and stir until thoroughly mixed. (Use absolutely level measuring tablespoons of flour since altered quantities produce biscuits which spread too far or not far enough!)

Stir the chopped nuts, cherries and peel into the butter, sugar and flour mixture.

Butter oven-slides, or by lining them with Teflon baking liners. Divide mixture in quarters. Form one quarter into four small balls and arrange on the tray, leaving plenty of space between them for spreading.

Bake in a pre-heated oven at 180°C for about 10 minutes, watching them carefully, in case they cook in a shorter time, eg. in a fan-assisted oven. The Florentines are ready when they have spread evenly, and are an even brown all over.

Take from oven and push uneven bits back into shape before the biscuits cool and firm up. When cool enough to lift, transfer them to a rack. When cold, carefully spread the flat underside of the Florentines with melted dark chocolate. When the chocolate coating is solid, transfer the biscuits to a shallow airtight container where they can be kept for a few days. The biscuits will soften if allowed to stand exposed to the air.

For a gourmet gift, package in an attractive container and decorate with curling ribbon etc.

Note: If biscuits do not spread to 6–7cm across, you used too much flour. Use 1 teaspoon less, next time!

Nut 'n' Ginger Macaroons

These small nutty biscuits keep for weeks and are perfect for nibbling after dinner or with afternoon tea or coffee. Pack them in a pretty glass jar for a special gift.

For 50 biscuits:

¾ cup sugar

150g hazelnuts or blanched almonds (or a
    mixture)

75g crystallised ginger, chopped

4 egg yolks

2 Tbsp vanilla sugar or caster sugar

1 tsp ground ginger (optional)

½ cup flour

1 teaspoon baking powder

pinch of salt

about 50 extra blanched almonds

Put the sugar and nuts in a food processor bowl and chop to a fine powder with the metal chopping blade. Add the roughly chopped ginger and process again until very fine. Remove from bowl.

Process the egg yolks, vanilla or caster sugar and ground ginger until light and fluffy. Add the ground nut mixture, flour, baking powder and salt and process well. The mixture should be quite firm.

Using wet hands, roll into about 50 balls, each about 1cm in diameter. Place on a baking tray lined with baking paper or a Teflon liner, and push a blanched almond on to the top of each ball.

Bake at 125°C in the centre of the oven for about 30 minutes. If biscuits do not harden on cooling, return to oven. Store in an airtight container. Flavour develops on standing.

Variation: Use 1½ cups ground almonds instead of the whole nuts. Leave out the flour in this case.

Almond Rosettes

For a present for someone special, fill a decorative glass jar, with a tight fitting lid, with these pretty biscuits. If you don't have a forcing bag, shape them by pushing them through a heavy weight plastic bag with the corner cut out.

For 24 - 36 biscuits:

2 egg whites
¼ cup plus 1 Tbsp caster sugar
125g ground almonds
¼–½ tsp almond essence
¼ tsp salt
8–16 glace cherries

Put the first five ingredients into a food processor. Mix until well blended and fairly smooth. If the mixture looks too soft to keep its shape at the end of this time, add more ground almonds.

Vary the amount of almond essence, depending on its strength. The biscuits should taste definitely, but not strongly, of almonds.

Spray an oven slide thickly with non-stick spray, or use a Teflon liner, since these biscuits stick easily. Pipe or otherwise shape them into rosettes, making 24–36 biscuits. As the biscuits do not rise during cooking, you can put them quite close together.

Cut the cherries into halves or quarters, and press them into the uncooked biscuit dough.

Bake at 180°C for about 20 minutes, until the biscuits are golden brown all over. If they appear to be browning too soon, turn the oven down to 170°C.

Cool on a rack, then store in airtight jars. These biscuits will stay nice and crisp for about a month if stored in an airtight container.

To make these without a food processor, beat the egg whites until bubbly but not stiff, add the remaining ingredients, and beat well with a wooden spoon until the mixture becomes quite stiff.

Custard Kisses

I could think of nothing nicer than being given a batch of small custard kisses as a gift—in a pretty box or jar, or packed as a Christmas Cracker in a tube. Lovely!

For 25 kisses:

175g butter
¾ cup icing sugar
1 tsp vanilla essence
1½ cups flour
½ cup custard powder
1 tsp baking powder

Icing:

2 Tbsp butter
½ cup icing sugar
1 Tbsp custard powder
few drops vanilla essence

Soften but do not melt butter. Cream with the icing sugar and vanilla then stir in the sifted flour, custard powder and baking powder. Mix well, then form the mixture into about fifty small balls. Flatten these in your hand before you put them on a lightly sprayed oven tray then make a pattern with a dampened fork, the dimpled surface of a meat hammer, or the bottom of a patterned glass.

OR form mixture into a cylinder and refrigerate until it will cut without flattening. Cut slices from the cylinder, put on a tray and decorate as above.

Bake at 170°–180°C for 12–15 minutes, depending on the thickness of the biscuits. When done they should feel firm, but should not have browned. Cool on a rack.

Stick cold biscuits together with icing made by mixing together softened (but not melted) butter and the other icing ingredients.

Store biscuits in airtight tins once the icing has set. Freeze if desired.

Rich Chocolate Log

This rich chocolate log should be thought of as candy. Keep it in the refrigerator and cut into thin slices before serving after dinner. Wrap in cellophane, like a cracker, when you give it as a gift.

½ of a (400g) can caramelised condensed milk

½ cup toasted almonds

½ cup toasted sunflower seeds OR toasted pumpkin seeds

½ cup walnuts

225g cooking chocolate

½ tsp vanilla essence

½ tsp rum essence (or more vanilla)

½ cup red and/or green cherries

½ cup dried fruit (chopped if large eg. dried apricots and prunes)

about 1 cup chopped toasted nuts for coating

Caramelise the condensed milk by simmering the can for 2 hours in a saucepan of water. (Keep can covered with water throughout the cooking time.)

Toast the nuts and seeds (on a shallow tray, 10cm from the grill) turning frequently until straw coloured.

Melt the chocolate either over hot water or on Medium in a microwave.

Measure the warm, caramelised condensed milk into a bowl, add the essences and stir to mix. Add the melted chocolate and stir well to combine. Stir in the nuts and fruit and mix well.

Tip the mixture out in a blobby sort of strip along a piece of plastic wrap about 75cm long. Fold the sides of the plastic together, then fold them over each other until you have the chocolate mixture enclosed in a plastic tube. Work with the chocolate mixture until it forms a long sausage as long as the plastic. Twist it in the centre to make two sausages, then again so you have four sausages.

Cut the plastic between the sausages and refrigerate until fairly firm. Unwrap each sausage and roll in chopped toasted nuts (any type you like) then re-wrap in plastic film. Wrap attractively, giving instructions for use.

To serve cut into thin slices with a serrated knife.

Note: Condensed milk may be caramelised months before you need it. Label carefully before storing it.

Lebkuchen

Try making these rock-hard Christmas Tree biscuits with your children. The uncooked dough tastes wonderful, so do not expect the impossible!

50g butter
1 cup honey
¾ cup brown sugar
1 Tbsp lemon juice
1 Tbsp finely grated lemon rind
2 tsp cinnamon
1 tsp ground cloves
1 tsp nutmeg
1 tsp allspice
½ tsp baking soda
3–4 cups flour

Measure all the ingredients except the baking soda and flour into a medium sized saucepan. Stir over a low heat until all the ingredients are blended and the sugar is no longer grainy. Do not boil. Remove from the heat and cool to room temperature.

Stir in the baking soda sifted with 1 cup of the flour. Stir well then add more flour, about half a cup at a time, until the dough is firm enough to roll out on a

floured board. The more flour you add, the harder and longer lasting the biscuits will be.

Roll out dough to about 5mm thick and cut into interesting shapes, using biscuit cutters etc. Before cooking, pierce a hole to thread red ribbon or wool through later. (A gently twisted straw makes good holes.)

Bake at 170°C for about 10–20 minutes, or longer, until the edges brown lightly. (Longer baked biscuits are harder.)

Cool on a rack. Leave plain or decorate as desired with water icing, or make an icing of piping consistency, adding water and a little butter to icing sugar, and pipe designs on to the cooked biscuits. If you don't have an icing nozzle, you can put your icing mixture into a strong plastic bag then snip a very small hole in one corner.

Painted Biscuits

Great fun for children to make for Christmas for Grandparents etc! These biscuits are cut into shapes then painted before they are baked. They look rather like animal biscuits, but are not quite as sweet.

100g butter
½ cup caster sugar
1 egg
½ tsp vanilla, almond or lemon essence
1½ cups flour
½ tsp baking powder

Beat the butter and caster sugar together until well mixed.

Separate the egg. Put the white in with the butter and sugar, and put the yolk aside in a small bowl or cup.

Add the essence after the egg white and stir well. Sift the flour and baking powder into this and stir until everything is mixed.

Put the dough in a cold place for five minutes, then roll out thinly on a floured board and cut into circles with a glass or into a variety of shapes using fancy cutters. (Dip cutters in flour so they do not stick to the mixture.)

Using a lightly floured fish slice or spatula, put the biscuits on an oven tray which as been lightly buttered, sprayed or covered with a Teflon liner. Handle carefully so you do not distort the shapes.

Stir the egg yolk with a fork and divide it into three parts, colour each part with food colouring, then paint the biscuits, using paint brushes. Turn round biscuits into happy/funny faces and paint simple or more complicated details to suit other shapes.

Bake at 170°–180°C for 5–10 minutes, until edges are very lightly browned. The time will depend on temperature and thickness of the dough.

Cool on a rack. When cold pack on pretty paper plates covered with plastic wrap so they are airtight.

"Stained Glass" Biscuits

These spectacular biscuits are fun to make with older children as a holiday project! Attractively wrapped they make an ideal present. They should be hung on a Christmas tree only if each is wrapped in plastic film so it is airtight.

225g butter
1¼ cups sugar
½ tsp baking soda
¼ cup water
3–4 cups flour
brightly coloured Lifesavers or other clear,
   coloured toffee-like sweets

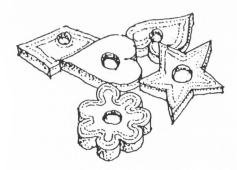

Soften but do not melt the butter. Add the sugar and cream thoroughly in a beater or food processor. Mix the baking soda and water, beat into the creamed mixture, then add the amount of flour you need.

If you intend to roll the mixture into a rope, then shape it by hand, add three cups of flour. Chill if the dough is too soft to work with, then roll small amounts into a rope about 7mm in diameter. Shape lengths of this into suitable outlines.

If you are going to roll out the mixture and cut shapes from it with cutters, add four cups of flour. Roll the dough out thinly then cut heart (or other) outlines, first using a larger cutter, then using a smaller cutter to remove the centre portion, leaving a space to fill with candy.

For biscuits to hang up later, cut a circular hole with a straw.

Place the biscuits on a Teflon non-stick baking sheet liner or on smooth, lightly buttered aluminium foil, and bake at 180°C for about 4 minutes. Remove from oven and sprinkle finely crushed coloured "Lifesavers" or other toffee-like sweets into the centre of each shaped biscuit. (Do not mix colours in the same biscuit.) Bake again for 2–3 minutes, until the toffee melts and bubbles, and the biscuit mixture is lightly coloured. Watch carefully during this time.

Remove from the oven and let the "glass" centre cool and harden before lifting the biscuits carefully from the tray.

Store or wrap immediately in airtight containers, or the toffee will become soft and sticky.

Christmas Tree Biscuits

These biscuits may be cut in interesting shapes and decorated so that they look really festive. You can hang them on a Christmas tree for a week or so.

150g butter
¼ tsp almond essence
1 tsp ground cardamom (optional)
½ cup caster sugar
1 egg, separated
2 Tbsp milk
about 2 cups flour

Cream the softened butter, essence, cardamom, and sugar together until light coloured and fluffy. Add the egg yolk and milk and beat again, then add enough flour to make a dough which is firm enough to roll out and cut in shapes.

Cut biscuits into different festive shapes with suitable cutters. If you do not have any special cutters, cut out large circles with a glass, then cut smaller circles from the centres of these using the tops of small bottles. For biscuits to hang up, cut a small circular hole with a straw before baking.

For almond wreath biscuits, beat the egg white with a fork until bubbly but not white, brush it onto the uncooked circles of dough, and arrange flaked almonds so they overlap, in a circular pattern. (The egg white acts as glue.)

Decorate other biscuits after baking.

Bake at 150°C for about 15 minutes, or until very lightly browned. Cool on a rack.

Make white icing by beating the remaining egg white with sifted icing sugar until mixture is of good spreading consistency. Spread icing with a small knife. Neaten iced edges by running a finger around biscuits after icing them. Decorate iced biscuits with slices of cherries, silver cachoux etc., before the icing hardens.

Attach biscuits to tree with silver or gold thread, or with tartan ribbons and fine wire, etc.

There is only one snag! Unwrapped biscuits do soften on the tree, and although they will last a couple of weeks, they are not good for eating after this time.

Forget about the tree altogether, if you like. Pack the decorated biscuits in a reusable glass container for gifts.

Christmas Pudding Truffles

I like these truffles dressed up so that they look like mini-Christmas puddings. If you feel that this is
too time-consuming, serve them as plain truffles rolled in coconut. They taste very good both ways.

1 cup currants
2 tsp very finely grated orange or tangelo
*   rind*
¼ cup rum, whisky, brandy or citrus juice
250g (2½ cups) crumbs from a chocolate
*   or plain cake*
125g (⅝ cup) chocolate chips
For decoration:
75 g white chocolate
1 tsp oil
about 6 red cherries
about 6 green cherries

Put the currants in a sieve and pour boiling water through them, then put them in a bowl with the very finely grated rind from a tangelo or orange, and the spirit of your choice or the same amount of juice from the orange or tangelo.

Leave the currants to stand while you crumb the cake, and then melt the chocolate chips, heating until liquid. This will take about 4–5 minutes on Medium in a Microwave oven, and a little longer in a large metal bowl standing over a pot of hot but not boiling water. When the chocolate has melted, stir into it the crumbs, then the currant mixture.

Mix well together, then roll into small, walnut sized balls, or balls which will fit nicely in small foil or fluted paper confectionery cups. (Roll in coconut if not decorating further.) Refrigerate until cold.

Warm pieces of white chocolate with the oil in a clean bowl, in a microwave oven for 3 minutes on Medium or over hot water, as before. Stir until smooth.

Chop the cherries. Have red cherry pieces chunky, and the green pieces pointed like leaves.

Spoon a little of the warm white mixture on top of a little pudding, helping it to look as if it is flowing, if necessary.

This takes a little experience, but is mainly a matter of having the truffle cold and the melted mixture semi-liquid. Before the white chocolate sets, put about three little red berries in the middle of the icing, and a couple of green leaves around them.

Christmas Pudding Truffles

Christmas Gift Box

Easy Christmas Confections

Let school-aged children help when you make uncooked confections. In next to no time they will be able to prepare them alone - although the final yield may not be quite as large as you thought!

Peanut Butter Squares

100g butter, cubed
½ cup peanut butter
1 cup wine biscuit crumbs
1 cup icing sugar
¼ tsp each almond and vanilla essence
100g white chocolate
2 tsp butter

Microwave butter and peanut butter on High for 2 minutes then stir thoroughly. (This can also be done in a pot over a low heat.) Add the biscuit crumbs, icing sugar and essences. Mix well and press into a shallow pan about 20 x 30cm, lined with baking paper.

Using gentle heat, melt the chocolate and the second measure of butter until they mix together smoothly. Spread on top of the chilled mixture and cut into small squares before the topping sets.

Fruity Nut Balls

1 cup each sultanas, walnuts, dates and
   cornflakes
orange juice, sherry or brandy
½ cup desiccated coconut
1 tsp cinnamon

Pour boiling water over sultanas in a sieve, drain well, then chop roughly in a food processor. Add walnuts and roughly chopped pitted dates, and process briefly. Add the cornflakes or other breakfast cereal, process again and moisten with the liquid of your choice, until the mixture is soft enough to form balls.

Roll into small balls with wet hands and drop into a bowl or plastic bag containing the coconut and cinnamon. Shake to coat.

Refrigerate or freeze.

Orange Fudge Squares

100g butter
½ of a (400g) can condensed milk
finely grated rind 1 orange
2 Tbsp orange juice
250g wine biscuits, finely crushed
about 36 walnut halves

Melt the butter then add the condensed milk and mix well in a bowl or a food processor. Stir in the rind, orange juice and crumbs them press into a 20cm square tin lined with baking paper. If you like, press freshly shelled walnut halves into the top of the warm fudge, in 6 rows. Refrigerate until set, then cut into 36 squares.

Refrigerate or freeze.

Note: Crush biscuits in a food processor or in a plastic bag with a rolling pin.

Chocolate Treats

These recipes will please all "chocoholics". Work your way up from my easy truffles, past my foolproof fudge to the delicious (if decadent) liqueur balls. Don't be surprised if the intended gifts disappear before they are packaged.

Chocolate Truffles

100g wine biscuit crumbs
100g butter
¼ cup cocoa
1 cup icing sugar
½ cup coconut
2 Tbsp sherry

Put the biscuits in a plastic bag and bang with a rolling pin until completely crushed.

Soften, but do not melt the butter. Add cocoa, icing sugar, coconut, sherry and the crushed biscuits. Stir well, and cool the mixture for 10 minutes in the refrigerator before rolling it into small balls.

Roll the balls in extra coconut.

Store in refrigerator or freezer.

Easy Chocolate Fudge

500g dark chocolate
400g can condensed milk
½ tsp vanilla
walnut halves to decorate (optional)

Break up the chocolate if necessary. Heat the condensed milk with the broken chocolate in a heavy pot, over a low heat, or in a microwave oven on Medium, stirring frequently until the chocolate is melted and the two are well blended.

Add the vanilla, stir well and pour into 20cm cake square pan lined with baking paper or a Teflon liner.

Leave until firm, then cut into 8 strips crosswise and lengthways. Top pieces with a walnut half if desired.

Cover and refrigerate or freeze.

Liqueur Balls

150g dark cooking chocolate
2 Tbsp orange flavoured liqueur
2 Tbsp butter
1 egg yolk
¼ cup cocoa

Break the chocolate up if necessary. Put into a microwaveable dish with your chosen liqueur. Heat for 3–4 minutes on Defrost until the chocolate is soft and will mix easily with the liqueur.

Add the butter and egg yolk and mix until well combined. (The warm chocolate will melt the butter). Leave aside for 3–4 hours at cool room temperature before rolling into walnut sized balls. Roll each ball in cocoa.

Store in refrigerator or freezer.

Fruity Favourites

Fruit is an important part of these confections, adding tanginess as well as sweetness.
All are long time favourites in our house.

Citrus Slice

100g butter
³⁄₄ cup condensed milk
1 cup coconut
grated rind of 1 or 2 citrus fruit
200g wine biscuits, crushed
1 cup icing sugar
2 Tbsp soft butter
citrus fruit juice

Melt the butter. Add condensed milk, coconut, finely grated rind of one large or two small lemons, oranges, mandarins or tangelos, and the finely crushed biscuit crumbs. Mix well, then press into a lightly buttered 20cm square tin.

Mix icing sugar with second measure of butter then stir in enough juice to make icing. Spread on slice, refrigerate until firm, then cut in small squares.

Apricot Balls

rind from ¹⁄₂ –1 orange
¹⁄₂ cup caster sugar
250g dried apricots, chopped
juice of ¹⁄₂ orange
1³⁄₄ cups desiccated coconut

Finely chop the peeled rind with the sugar in a food processor, then add the apricots and process until all is finely chopped. Make the orange juice up to ¹⁄₄ cup with either lemon juice, sherry or brandy then add and process briefly again.

Add a cup of the coconut, process, then add extra coconut until mixture sticks together nicely. With wet hands form into small balls, and coat with the remaining coconut.

Refrigerate uncovered until firm. (Freeze if desired.)

Cherry Truffles

200g wine biscuits, crushed
1¹⁄₂ cups coconut
12–20 glace cherries
100g melted butter
¹⁄₂ of a (400g) can condensed milk
1 tsp almond essence (optional)
¹⁄₄ cup sherry, brandy or kirsch

Crush biscuits until fine. Mix crumbs with the coconut and the chopped cherries.

Heat the butter in a small pan until liquid. Remove from heat and add condensed milk. Add almond essence if you are not using the kirsch. Stir in the sherry, brandy or kirsch, then pour mixture into crumbs and coconut and mix well.

Roll into small balls, and coat with extra coconut. Refrigerate or freeze.

Mouthwatering Morsels

Let your children make my foolproof Coconut Ice for someone special — encourage them to help shape and colour Marzipan Fruit — then reward yourself with my Fabulous Fudge!

Uncooked Coconut Ice

½ of a (400g) can condensed milk
2 cups desiccated coconut
2 cups icing sugar
1 tsp vanilla essence
¼ tsp raspberry essence
4–6 drops red food colouring

Warm can of condensed milk if cold. Measure into fairly large bowl (or food processor bowl). Add coconut, icing sugar and vanilla. Mix until combined.

Remove half mixture and press out 1 cm thick on extra coconut on board. To remaining mixture, add raspberry essence and enough colouring to make a medium pink. Press this over the white layer. Chill until firm for 15–30 minutes, then cut into squares.

Refrigerate or freeze.

Marzipan Fruits

Make one quantity of Homemade Almond Icing (see page 6). Divide the dough into four parts and leave one part uncoloured. With food colouring, colour one part red, one part blue and one part yellow. Mix these together to make fruit colours.

Gently shape small balls of marzipan to form strawberries, pears, bananas, apples and oranges. Intensify the colours of the fruit by painting with more food colouring.

Use the cloves and cocoa to decorate the fruits. Push cloves in to the ends to make stalks and paint brown areas on bananas with the cocoa mixed to a paste with water.

Fabulous Fudge

100g butter
1 cup sugar
¼ cup golden syrup
400g can condensed milk
1 tsp vanilla

Mix all ingredients except vanilla in a microwave bowl resistant to high heat.

Microwave on High for 10–12 minutes, stirring every 2 minutes until all sugar has dissolved, mixture has bubbled vigorously all over surface, and a little dropped in cold water forms a soft ball.

Add vanilla. Beat for about 5 minutes, until mixture loses its gloss. Before it sets firm, spoon into a lightly buttered or sprayed 20cm square pan. When firm, cut into squares.

Chocolate-Coated Delights

I am still surprised when I see how "professional" my chocolate "goodies" look. Be prepared
for a little trial and error — the end results will be worth it.

Easy Peppermint Creams

25g butter
¼ cup condensed milk
½ tsp peppermint essence
about 2 cups icing sugar
green food colouring (optional)

Have butter soft but not melted. Mix first four ingredients in medium-sized bowl or food processor, adding enough icing sugar to form a firm paste.

Colour green, if desired. Shape into one or two rolls, wrap in plastic then chill until firm. Cut in slices to serve.

Dip chilled peppermint creams in melted chocolate if desired. Store chocolate-coated peppermints at room temperature, but uncoated creams in refrigerator.

Bulls' Eyes

1 cup freshly roasted peanuts
50g soft butter
¾ cup icing sugar
½ tsp almond or vanilla essence
1–3 Tbsp orange juice or sherry
100g cooking chocolate

Chop peanuts in food processor until very fine. Drop in butter, then add the icing sugar and essence. When well mixed, add enough orange juice or sherry to make mixture of rolling consistency. Form 20–30 balls, then chill.

Melt cooking chocolate in a small bowl over hot water. Submerge balls into melted chocolate leaving a circle on each uncovered.

Chill on a plastic-covered tray until set. Store in one layer in refrigerator.

Best Ever Chocolates

½ cup double cream
180–200g dark chocolate
50g butter, cubed
½ cup coconut cream
¼ tsp rum (or other) essence
200g cooking chocolate, broken into pieces

Heat the cream. Stir in chocolate and butter and mix until smooth. Add coconut cream and essence. (For fruity fillings, dissolve ⅛ teaspoon citric acid in ¼ teaspoon water. Add a little of this with fruit-flavoured essence to taste.)

Refrigerate for several hours, until firm. Shape into small squares or balls. Chill or freeze these.

Dip cold fillings into second measure of melted chocolate. When set, decorate with a thin stream of chocolate.

Marshmallows

When you make economical marshmallows, a few basic ingredients go a long way because of the amount of air beaten through the mixture.

2 Tbsp gelatine
1/2 cup cold water
2 cups sugar
3/4 cup hot water
1 tsp vanilla essence
pinch salt
1 cup coconut (toasted if desired)

Stir the gelatine into the cold water and leave it to stand. Boil the sugar and hot water in a medium-sized pot for about 15 minutes, until a little, dropped in cold water, forms a ball which can be flattened when squeezed. Stir the softened gelatine into this.

Stand pot in cold water until you can rest your hand on saucepan bottom. Add vanilla and salt and beat until thick and white using an electric beater. Pour the white fluffy mixture into a buttered or sprayed 20cm square cake tin.

Refrigerate several hours or overnight, then lift marshmallow out, warming tin slightly if necessary, on to a board sprinkled with plain or toasted coconut. Cut in squares and shake in more coconut, dampening squares with water if coconut doesn't stick at first. Eat within a few days.

Variation: Colour half the mixture pink and flavour with raspberry or strawberry essence.

Note: The boiled sugar and water mixture is too hot for young children to work with.

Butterballs and Candy Canes

This is my favourite toffee recipe. The partly cooled mix may be pulled into a pearly rope and cut into pieces, or shaped into Christmas Candy Canes. This recipe requires some speed, dexterity and adult supervision.

Butterballs

½ cup sugar
2 Tbsp water
2 Tbsp honey
2 Tbsp butter
½ tsp rum essence

Gently heat the sugar and water in a small pot until the sugar dissolves. Add the honey and butter and boil mixture gently without stirring. At intervals drop a few drops of the mixture into cold water. When the drops are hard, and crack when bitten, take pot off the heat and cool a little.

While you wait, rub a fairly thick layer of butter on to a shallow metal pan. Stir rum essence gently into the cooling candy, and pour it on to the buttery plate. When mixture is firm enough, lift edges towards centre.

When cool enough to handle, lift with buttered hands and stretch and twist several times to form a rope. Keep stretching and twisting mixture as it cools.

When firm, cut in short lengths with a heavy knife or buttered kitchen scissors

Store in an airtight container when cold.

Christmas Candy Canes

Make a double quantity of the toffee recipe above, but instead of using rum essence, divide the cooked mixture in half and flavour one half with peppermint essence and the other with raspberry essence, adding a few drops of red flavouring to the raspberry half.

Pull the toffee as described above, keeping the two colours separate.

To shape the canes, twist together two warm pulled strands, of different colours to form a rope. Cut in suitable lengths and bend tops into walking stick shapes.

Store in individual zip-lock bags, or wrap each cane separately in plastic film.

Brandied Fruit

Brandied Fruit makes a special dessert, alone or with cream or icecream. If the price of jars of commercially prepared fruit frightens you, make your own!

You can brandy any fruit you bottle conventionally. I have made brandied peaches, apricots, pineapple, pitted cherries, boysenberries and loganberries.

Pack the fruit in small decorative jars which hold about 1–1½ cups, with lacquered metal lids. When you want a gift, simply take a jar from your cupboard, polish it until it shines, and cover its top with a pinked circle of gingham (or granny print) secured with a rubber band then a ribbon. Attach a little card giving a few particulars of the contents of the jar and your troubles are over!

Pack the prepared fruit into thoroughly cleaned jars all of the same height. Add suitable whole spices if you like. Spoon 2–3 tablespoons of brandy (or light rum) into each jar. Fill jars to 1cm from the top with heavy syrup made by boiling one cup of sugar with one cup of water. Place

lids loosely on jars so air can escape during processing.

Place jars on a rack or crumpled foil in a large pot and add bath-temperature water up to the necks of the jars (boiling water might break the jars). Cover the pot. Bring to a gentle boil and process for 20 minutes, after the water comes to the boil.

After this, working quickly, ladle out some of the water and lift the jars one at a time onto a wooden board or a pad of newspapers. Quickly tighten the lids and leave to cool away from draughts.

Check that lids have sealed (centres should be concave) and store in a cool dry place until required.

Christmas Tree Biscuits

Christmas Mince Pies

Microwaved Pot Pourri

At Christmas time it is good to have something from your garden to give to close friends. I think it is a nice idea to walk around your garden, picking scented flowers and herbs with a friend in mind. After all, Pot Pourri will last much longer than fresh flowers do.

Pot Pourri is quickly made if you have a microwave oven. As well, most microwaved flowers and leaves look brighter than they do when conventionally dried.

(For large quantities of Pot Pourri, you can dry most of the petals conventionally, but you can then mix them with small amounts of the brighter, microwaved ones.)

Buy some dried, powdered orris root. Some chemists stock it, or will get it for you. Orris root is a "fixative". Flowers and leaves dried after a light coating of orris root keep their scent for a long time.

Flower oils boost the fragrance of your Pot Pourri, but you may finish up with unnaturally strong-smelling mixtures if you add them without care and restraint.

My Pot Pourris are usually based on scented rose petals and lavender with small amounts of other additions. I have used rosemary flowers and leaves, violet flowers, carnation petals, catmint and catnip flowers and leaves, gorse flowers, sweet peas, lemon-scented verbena leaves, leaves and flowers from thyme, marjoram, and lemon balm. I sometimes add calendula, blue love-in-the-mist, cornflowers and delphiniums for colour.

Keep each flower variety separate. Break large flowers into petals and take leaves from the stems. Spread small amounts of each type on to a folded paper towel.

Sprinkle with orris root and turn flowers and leaves to coat, using one teaspoon per half cup of flower petals. Cover with another paper towel.

Microwave on High until the petals are dry, but not crisp enough to crumble. The time will vary from 30 seconds to 2 or 3 minutes, depending on quantity and moisture. (Watch carefully, since overdried flowers can brown, or may even catch fire.) Once the petals are dried, mix them with a little extra orris root and a pinch of salt.

To add spiciness, choose several of the following: finely grated orange and lemon rind, freshly grated nutmeg, crushed coriander seeds, broken cinnamon stick, crushed cloves, and slivers of a vanilla pod. Mix well. Leave the Pot Pourri in a bowl or other open container for one to two weeks, stirring or shaking them at intervals. When quite dry, pack into pretty containers.

Nuts to Nibble

When you roast nuts yourself, you can add interesting flavours and make your gift — or snack — unique. Always start with best quality nuts. If you like, try these recipes with other types of nuts such as pecans, cashews or hazelnuts.

Curried Walnuts

1 cup (100g) walnut halves
1 tsp olive or other oil
½ tsp salt
½ tsp curry powder
½ tsp caster sugar

Boil the walnuts in two cups of water for 2–3 minutes, drain off water immediately and pat nuts dry between layers of paper towel.

Drizzle the oil over the nuts in a shallow bowl, then mix gently with your fingers to coat evenly. Place flat sides down on a Teflon liner or on baking paper on an oven slide.

Mix salt, curry powder and caster sugar and sprinkle evenly over nuts. (For even coating, shake through a fine sieve.)

Bake at 125°C for 15–20 minutes, then transfer to a paper towel to cool.

When cold, pack into hot, dry, airtight jars or thoroughly sealed plastic or cellophane bags.

Devilled Almonds

1 cup (150g) almonds
1 tsp olive or other oil
1 tsp light soya sauce
1 tsp Tabasco sauce
½ tsp each garlic and celery salt
½ tsp curry powder
½ tsp 5 spice powder (optional)
pinch cayenne pepper (optional)

Toss the almonds, oil, soya and Tabasco sauces together in a large bowl. Leave to stand for 5 minutes.

Mix remaining flavourings adding the cayenne pepper if you want extra "heat". Sprinkle this mixture over the nuts, tossing to coat evenly.

Spread on a Teflon liner or baking paper on an oven slide.

Bake at 125°C for 15 minutes.

When cool pack in screw-topped jars or in plastic or cellophane bags.

Nuts to Nibble

A nicely decorated jar of carefully seasoned, roasted nuts is always a welcome gift. Choose your decorations and seasonings to suit the recipient!

Spiced Almonds

1 cup (150g) almonds
2 tsp egg white
¼ cup caster sugar
1 tsp cinnamon
1 tsp mixed spice
¼ tsp ground cloves
pinch salt

Put the (dry) nuts into a large bowl. Add the measured egg white which has been beaten very lightly with a fork.

Using your fingers, coat the nuts with the egg. Leave to stand for 4–5 minutes, until the nuts soak up some of the egg and have only a "tacky" surface.

Meanwhile mix the caster sugar with the remaining ingredients. Put half of this mixture in with the nuts, shake to coat lightly then arrange nuts in one layer on a Teflon liner or baking paper on an oven slide.

Shake or finely sieve more coating mixture over nuts (do not turn nuts over).

Bake at 125°C (without fan if possible) for 15 minutes. When cool transfer to airtight jars, plastic or cellophane bags.

Caramel Orange Almonds

1 cup (150g) blanched almonds
rind of 1 orange, very finely grated
1 tsp orange juice
½ tsp vanilla essence
½ tsp citric acid
about ¼ cup caster sugar

Toss the almonds in a dry bowl with the very finely grated orange rind, orange juice, vanilla and citric acid. When evenly coated leave to stand in the bowl for five minutes.

Toss with half of the caster sugar, then without handling, tip onto an oven slide covered with a Teflon liner or baking paper.

Sprinkle the remaining sugar over the nuts on the tray. Do not turn or stir.

Bake at 125°C for 15–20 minutes, watching carefully. When the sugar melts and the nuts are golden, remove from the oven.

When cold, pack in airtight jars, cellophane or plastic bags.

Christmas Pickle

I named this pickle for its festive colours. I often give it to friends at Christmas, as it tastes so good with cold meats. It turns cheese and crackers into something special, and is useful when unexpected guests call.

8 cups diced telegraph cucumber
¼ cup plain salt
4 onions, diced
2–3 red peppers, diced
3 cups sugar
1 tsp celery seed
1 tsp mustard seed
2 cups wine vinegar
2–3 Tbsp cornflour

Halve cucumbers lengthwise then scoop out the central seedy part, using a teaspoon. Without removing peel, cut cucumber flesh into small, evenly shaped cubes.

Measure cucumber into a glass, plastic china or stainless steel container. Sprinkle with salt and leave to stand for 30 minutes, stirring several times. Drain and rinse, discarding liquid.

Cut the onions and peppers into cubes the same size as the cucumber. Put prepared cucumber, onion, peppers, sugar, celery and mustard seeds and vinegar into a large saucepan. Bring to the boil stirring constantly. Mix cornflour with a little extra vinegar and stir into the cucumber mixture.

Pour into hot jars that have been cleaned and heated in the oven. If jars have plastic screw lids or lacquered metal lids, pour boiling water over them and leave to stand for a few minutes, then screw them on to the hot jars of pickle.

For jars without lids, cover cool pickle with melted paraffin (or candle) wax, then with cellophane tops.

Notes: A 2 litre icecream container holds exactly 8 cups of cubed cucumber.

Pickles which are stored in the refrigerator do not need to be sealed.

Bread 'n' Butter Pickles

These pickles have become part of my annual preserving list and friends are always delighted when I give them a jar, as a gift from my kitchen. As their name suggests, they are a great addition to bread-based snacks and sandwiches.

2 litres sliced cucumber
½–1 litre sliced onion
½ cup salt
3 cups wine vinegar
1 Tbsp mustard seeds
1 Tbsp celery seed
1 tsp turmeric

For preference use immature (or telegraph) cucumbers which have soft skins and which are not soft and watery in the middle.

Slice the unpeeled cucumbers and the peeled onions thinly into 2 litre icecream containers for easy measuring. Sprinkle with salt, cover with cold water and leave to stand for 8–12 hours, then discard the salty liquid, rinse with cold water and drain well.

In a large pot or jam pan, heat the vinegar, seeds and turmeric. When the mixture boils add the drained vegetables. As soon as the mixture comes back to the boil, ladle the vegetables and liquid into clean sterilised jars. Fill nearly to overflowing and seal immediately with seals (or screw-on, lacquered metal lids)

that have been boiled for five minutes. Screw on bands if used. Remove bands when pickles are quite cold. (Do not tighten or disturb screwed on lids.)

Wipe jars and store in a cool dark place for up to a year.

After jars have been open, store in the refrigerator.

Note: When filling jars, make sure all the liquid is used, evenly distributed. The contents of jars without enough vinegar may spoil.

Maharajah's Chutney

I invented this Indian-style chutney a few years ago. It is delicious, unusual and very popular with my family and friends. Try it on crackers with or without cheese.

10 plump cloves garlic, chopped
500g onions, chopped
2 tsp grated fresh ginger
1 Tbsp black mustard seed
5 small dried chilies
3 Tbsp coriander seed
2 Tbsp cumin seed, crushed
1 Tbsp cinnamon
2 tsp turmeric
½ cup oil
2 Tbsp salt
2 cups malt vinegar
2 cups sugar
500g sultanas, roughly chopped
2 lemons, grated rind and juice

Chop the garlic and quartered onions into pea-sized pieces in a food processor or with a knife. Mix with the ginger in a large bowl.

Using a pestle and mortar, a coffee and spice grinder or a heavy duty plastic bag and a hammer, break up the next four ingredients together. Heat them in a large, heavy-based pot until fragrant, stir in the cinnamon and turmeric, and heat through. Add about half the oil, then the onion mixture, and cook for about 5 minutes until transparent but not browned.

Measure and add remaining ingredients, including the rest of the oil, chopping the sultanas in a food processor or with a knife. Bring chutney mixture to the boil and simmer for about 1 hour, stirring frequently to prevent sticking.

Pour hot chutney into clean heated jars, and top immediately with boiled screw-on metal lids. If chutney is to be refrigerated, it need not be in sealed jars. Label with its name and suggested uses.

Hot Tangy Mustard

Packed in small decorative jars, this mustard makes a lovely Christmas gift from your kitchen. Jars of mustard do not need to be heat sealed so you can top them with glass lids, plastic screw tops, corks or metal lids with lacquered insides.

½ cup yellow mustard seed
¼ cup black mustard seed
1 Tbsp green peppercorns
1 Tbsp fresh tarragon leaves
2 tsp salt
½ cup wine vinegar
½ cup dry vermouth or sherry
½ cup olive or other oil

Put all ingredients except the oil into a food processor and process with the metal chopping blade until some of the mustard grains break up and the liquid thickens and turns cloudy.

Add the oil gradually with the motor still running.

Leave for at least 24 hours for the mustard grains to soften and for the flavour to develop. If you want a thicker, smoother mixture, process again at this stage. Taste and alter the seasonings if you like.

Variation: If you like a milder, more tangy mustard, you can use this hot, strong mustard as a base. Put quarter of a cup of the mustard above into the food processor

with two tablespoons of wine vinegar and quarter of a teaspoon of salt. With the motor running, add quarter of a cup of olive oil in a thin stream. Bottle the resulting mixture and store in a cool place. This mixture may separate if kept longer than a few days.

Herbed Vinegars and Spiced Oil

Vinegars flavoured with summer herbs make attractive gifts. These and spiced oil are useful in winter months when the fresh herbs and other flavourings are not readily available. Top and label the jars attractively, suggesting uses for the contents.

Tarragon Vinegar

Chop up enough fresh tarragon stalks and leaves to fill half a cup. Put in a jar with 1–2 cups wine vinegar. Add a chili, a clove of garlic, and/or some peppercorns, cover, and leave in a warm place for about two weeks. Taste, add a little salt and sugar if you like, then strain into an attractive bottle containing one or more tarragon sprigs.

Use in mayonnaise, other salad dressings and Bernaise Sauce.

Dill Vinegar

Make this in the same way as you would tarragon vinegar, using dill seed heads, flower and bud heads, and leaves. Put the chopped pieces in the jar with a few nasturtium leaves, seeds, and/or buds, if desired. Cover, shake at intervals for a week, then strain, and rebottle with dill flowers or seed heads and a few nasturtium flowers. These will keep their colour, but not shape.

Especially nice in salads containing cucumber and in fish sauces.

Lavender Vinegar

Fill a jar with the heads of flowering English lavender. Cover with white wine vinegar, and leave in a warm place, away from direct sunlight for two or three days. Pour off the vinegar, which will be a startling purple, put more lavender flowers into the jar with the old ones and cover with more vinegar. Leave in a warm place for about a week, then pour off the liquid and mix with the earlier lavender vinegar. Add a few fresh sprigs of lavender for decoration.

Lovely with tomato salads or as a facial splash!

Strawberry Vinegar

Pour wine vinegar over clean, ripe, but not mushy berries in a jar, covering them generously. Cover and stand in a dark place at room temperature. Pour off the liquid after about 2–4 weeks, leaving any sediment behind. The colour fades with time, but the flavour remains.

Sprinkle over strawberries or use in dressings for green salads and avocados.

Spiced Olive Oil

Three-quarters fill an attractive bottle with your favourite olive oil. Thread on one or two skewers several cloves of garlic and one or more varieties of whole or halved fresh red and/or green chilis. Cut skewers to fit the bottles and lower in carefully. Top bottles with more oil.

Used spiced oil in dressings and when sauteeing meat and vegetables, refilling bottle with fresh oil as the flavoured oil is used.

Variation: For an elusive smoky flavour, add chipotle (smoked) chilis, if you can find them.

Important Information

For best results use a standard metric (250ml) cup and standard metric spoons when using the recipes in this book.

    1 metric teaspoon holds 5ml
    1 metric tablespoon holds 15ml

All the cup and spoon measures are level, unless otherwise stated. (Rounded or heaped measures will upset the balance of ingredients.)

When measuring flour, spoon it into the measure lightly, and level it off without shaking or banging the cup, since this packs down the flour and means that too much is used. Small ¼ and ½ cup measures are useful for measuring these quantities of flour.

Most butter quantities are given by weight. Small amounts of butter are measured by tablespoon. 1 tablespoonful weighs 15 grams.

cm	centimetre
g	gram
C	Celsius
ml	millilitre
kg	kilogram
l	litre

Microwave cooking times vary, and cannot be given precisely. Microwave instructions have been given for a 650 watt microwave oven with a turntable.

High	100% power
Medium	50% power
Medium High	70% power
Defrost	30% power

Use large eggs unless otherwise stated.

Acknowledgements

The recipes in this book have been tested and made with the following products:

ALISON'S CHOICE for dried fruit, nuts, grains, seeds and cereals.

BENNICKS POULTRY FARM, Levin, for fresh eggs.

EMERSON'S BOUTIQUE BREWERY, Grange St Dunedin, for beer and ales.

EMPIRE FOODSTUFFS, for spices and dried herbs.

HARKNESS AND YOUNG LTD, for Probus utensils and Willow non-stick cookware.

J WATTIE FOODS, for canned fruit.

LAMNEI PLASTICS, PO Box 30405, Lower Hutt, for Alison Holst's Microwave Dishes.

NESTLE NEW ZEALAND LTD, for chocolate and condensed milk.

RICHMOND FOODS, for New Way Pastry.

S.C. JOHNSON & SON, for Chef Mate cooking spray.

SUREBRAND, Auckland, for Teflon non-stick cake tin and oven tray liners.

TIMOS, for Filo Pastry

WILLIAM AITKEN & CO LTD, Wellington, for Azalea Grapeseed Oil and Lupi Olive Oils.

Index

Index

Knives by Mail Order

For the past 17 years I have imported my favourite, very sharp kitchen knives from Switzerland. These keep their edges well, are easy to sharpen, and a pleasure to use. These knives are extremely sharp. Please use them with care until you are used to this!

VEGETABLE KNIFE $8.00 Pointed, straight edged, 85mm blade, in a plastic sheath. Useful for peeling vegetables and cutting small objects.

UTILITY KNIFE $9.00 Pointed 103mm blade which slopes back, in a plastic sheath. Use for boning chicken and meat and general kitchen use.

SERRATED KNIFE $9.00 Rounded end, 110mm serrated knife in a plastic sheath. This never needs sharpening, will stay sharp for years, and is unbelievably useful for slicing steak, bread and fresh baking, tomatoes and fruit, etc.

THREE PIECE SET $17.00 Serrated knife (as above), 85mm blade vegetable knife with pointed tip, and (right-handed) potato peeler, all with black dishwasher-proof handles, together in a white plastic pack.

GIFT BOX KNIFE SETS $38.00 Five knives and a (right-handed) potato peeler. Contains straight bladed vegetable knife, blade 85mm; serrated edged vegetable knife, blade 85mm; small utility knife with a pointed tip blade 85mm; small serrated utility 85mm; larger rounded end serrated knife 110mm (same as above). ("Straight edge" means that blade is in line with handle.) Attractive pack.

SERRATED CARVING KNIFE $25.00 Cutting edge 21 cm, overall length 33 cm. Black, moulded dishwasher-proof handle. Cuts beautifully, and does not require sharpening. (Sharpening wears down the serrations.) In sheath.

STEEL $20.00 20 cm blade, 34 cm total length, black dishwasher-proof handle. Produces excellent results.

KNIFE SHARPENER $30.00 This sits on a bench, and is held safely, without slipping, with one hand while you draw a CLEAN knife (of any length) through it with your other hand. Easy to use, with two rotating sharpening disks of synthetic ruby. When knife is held vertically, discs are at ideal angle to sharpen it to a fine point. Dishwasher-proof. Do not use with serrated knives. This is excellent if you have trouble using a steel efficiently.

For each order (any number of knives) please add $3.00 for packing and postage. All prices include GST. These prices apply until the end of 1995.

Please send cheque with your order to:

Alison Holst Mail Orders
PO Box 17016
Wellington